SELF-DEFENSE
NERVE CENTERS & PRESSURE POINTS is based
on modern concepts of self-defense; the point of
view is ethical, humanistic and rational.

The results of self-defense actions are described in
the most accurate way possible, taking into account
the factors of relative size, strength, health and
emotional control.

Current knowledge of physiology and anatomy is
applied to this subject which has long been much
obscured by superstition, myth and legend. The
facts and the fantasies of the "deadly" blows are
examined and evaluated.

Appropriate body targets for practical self-defense
are compared with point targets used in stylized
martial arts and in sport tournament.

For the teacher and student of self-defense or of
any style of any specialty of the martial arts this
book is an important reference source.

"... *a practical guide to the most*
*effective weaponless self-defense*
*using the least possible force...*"

THE POLICE CHIEF

**BOOKS by BRUCE TEGNER**

BRUCE TEGNER'S COMPLETE BOOK of SELF-DEFENSE

SELF-DEFENSE: A BASIC COURSE

SELF-DEFENSE NERVE CENTERS & PRESSURE POINTS

DEFENSE TACTICS for LAW ENFORCEMENT
Weaponless Defense & Control and Baton Techniques

STICK-FIGHTING: SELF-DEFENSE

STICK-FIGHTING: SPORT FORMS

KUNG FU & TAI CHI

SAVATE: FRENCH FOOT & FIST FIGHTING

KARATE & JUDO EXERCISES

BRUCE TEGNER'S COMPLETE BOOK of JUJITSU

JUDO: BEGINNER to BLACK BELT

KARATE: BEGINNER to BLACK BELT

AIKIDO & BOKATA

**BOOKS by BRUCE TEGNER & ALICE McGRATH**

SELF-DEFENSE & ASSAULT PREVENTION for
   GIRLS & WOMEN

SELF-DEFENSE for YOUR CHILD
Elementary school age boys & girls

SOLO FORMS of KARATE, TAI CHI, AIKIDO
   & KUNG FU

**BOOKS by Ellen Kei Hua**

KUNG FU MEDITATIONS & Chinese Proverbial Wisdom

WISDOM from the EAST

MEDITATIONS of the MASTERS

# SELF-DEFENSE
## NERVE CENTERS & PRESSURE POINTS
### FOR KARATE, JUJITSU & ATEMI-WAZA

By BRUCE TEGNER

THOR PUBLISHING COMPANY
VENTURA CA 93002

**Library of Congress Cataloging in Publication Data**

Tegner, Bruce.
    Self-defense nerve centers & pressure points: for karate,
jujitsu & atemi-waza.

    Includes index
    1. Self-defense. I. Title.
GV1111.T423 1978     796.8'15     78-18169
ISBN 0-87407-519-X
ISBN 0-87407-029-5 pbk.

SELF-DEFENSE NERVE CENTERS & PRESSURE POINTS

First edition: September 1968
Second printing: October 1970
Third printing: April 1973
Fourth printing: December 1973
Fifth printing: February 1974
Sixth printing: March 1975
Enlarged, revised edition:  September  1978
Second printing:  April  1979
Third printing:  August  1980
Fourth printing:  April  1982
Fifth printing:  September  1982
Sixth printing:  August  1983
Seventh printing:  May  1984
Eighth printing:  July  1985

SELF-DEFENSE NERVE CENTERS & PRESSURE POINTS
For Karate, Jujitsu & Atemi-waza

Copyright © 1968, 1978 by Bruce Tegner & Alice McGrath

THOR PUBLISHING COMPANY
P.O. BOX 1782
VENTURA,  CA  93002                    PRINTED IN U.S.A.

ACKNOWLEDGMENTS
The material for this book was collected over many
years with the help of many people. My students, and
friends in civilian and military police work provided
personal observations and reports, for which I am
grateful.

The late V. E. Christensen, M.D. helped me in the
preparation of an earlier version of this book by
assisting me in researching accident and injury reports
and by allowing me to observe and question him
during post-mortem examinations. Dr. Christensen
had an active interest in sports medicine. He had
studied kung fu and aikido and he held a black belt
rank in karate. He was a valuable consultant and
a valued friend. He is remembered with appreciation
and affection.

For the present version I have had the assistance of
H. O'Neil Zeigler, an instructor of comparative
anatomy and physiology, who gave suggestions for
updating the material, and of Dick Schumacher,
whose specialty is evaluation of sport-related injury.
I am grateful to them for useful discussions and
comments and for their generosity and kindness.

Most of the photos illustrating the striking
areas are of RICHARD WINDISHAR.

The photos showing some examples of
defense actions are taken from:
*BRUCE TEGNER'S COMPLETE BOOK of SELF-DEFENSE*
*SELF-DEFENSE for YOUR CHILD*

*SELF-DEFENSE & ASSAULT PREVENTION for*
        *GIRLS & WOMEN*
all of which are published by Thor Publishing Company,
Ventura, California.

Drawings on pages 114,116,117 and 119 are
by    KEVIN MILLER

# BRUCE TEGNER BOOKS REVIEWED

**KARATE: BEGINNER to BLACK BELT**
"Techniques and routines...illustrated in profuse detail...a fine introduction and a worthwhile reference source...specially geared to a YA audience."     KLIATT YOUNG ADULT PB BOOK GUIDE

**SELF-DEFENSE: A BASIC COURSE**
"An eminently practical, concise guide to self-defense...for young men..."     American Library Association BOOKLIST

"YA - A calm, nonsexist approach to simple yet effective self-defense techniques...clear photographs...sound advice."     SCHOOL LIBRARY JOURNAL

**BRUCE TEGNER'S COMPLETE BOOK OF JUJITSU**
"...authoritative and easy-to-follow text..."     SCHOOL LIBRARY JOURNAL

**BRUCE TEGNER'S COMPLETE BOOK OF SELF-DEFENSE**
Recommended for Y.A. in the American Library Association     BOOKLIST

**SELF-DEFENSE & ASSAULT PREVENTION FOR GIRLS & WOMEN (with Alice McGrath)**
"...should be required reading for all girls and women..."     WILSON LIBRARY BULLETIN

"...simple and straightforward with no condescension...easy to learn and viable as defense tactics..."     SCHOOL LIBRARY JOURNAL

**SELF-DEFENSE FOR YOUR CHILD (with Alice McGrath)**
[For elementary school-age boys & girls]
"...informative, readable book for family use..."     CHRISTIAN HOME & SCHOOL

**DEFENSE TACTICS FOR LAW ENFORCEMENT**
"...a practical tool for police academy programs, police programs at the university level, and for the (individual) officer..."     THE POLICE CHIEF

**KUNG FU & TAI CHI: Chinese Karate and Classical Exercise**
"...recommended for physical fitness collections."     LIBRARY JOURNAL

**SOLO FORMS of Karate, Tai Chi, Aikido & Kung Fu (with Alice McGrath)**
"...well-coordinated, step-by-step instructions...carefully captioned photos...for personal enjoyment and exercise..." YA     American Library Association BOOKLIST

**STICK-FIGHTING: SPORT FORMS**
"...illustrations and directions are clear and easy to follow... based on foil fencing, quarterstaff and broadsword...in addition to sports-oriented use...might prove of value to drama students..."     American Library Association BOOKLIST

# CONTENTS

**INTRODUCTION** by ALICE McGRATH

## NERVE CENTERS & PRESSURE POINTS

## SUPPLEMENT

# INTRODUCTION

## WHAT IS SELF-DEFENSE?

A modern definition of self-defense is in order. One way of defining self-defense is to explain what it is *not*. Personal self-defense is not warfare; it is not vengeance; it is not an art; it is not a sporting event; it is not a movie or television fight scene.

Self-defense is preparation to minimize the possibility of assault. It is training to learn and use appropriate and effective physical actions if there is no practical available alternative.

Self-defense instruction is the beginning of a process of learning how to avoid becoming a victim.

Many victims of assault are victims not because they lack the capacity to win fights but because they have been given absolutely no preparation to cope with this special kind of emergency.

The old-fashioned view that self-defense instruction is training to reach a high level of fighting skill has the effect of eliminating those individuals who have the greatest need. It is precisely those people who are unable or unwilling to become fierce fighting machines who benefit from practical self-defense instruction to the greatest degree.

Our capabilities ought to bear some relationship to real-life objectives. People learning to defend themselves against assault ought not to be trained as though they were preparing for warfare. The concepts, techniques and methods appropriate for training Samurai warriors are not those appropriate for teaching self-defense as a practical skill for today.

The legal and moral definition of self-defense expressly limits the degree of force to the *least* which can be used to avert, stop, or escape from an intended assault.

In old-style self-defense, every assault is viewed as a very vicious assault. Real life is different. There are degrees of

danger. Assault intentions range from mildly threatening
to the intent to do great bodily harm. More important,
there are mildly threatening situations which, if handled
properly with assertive self-control, can be prevented
from escalating into physical violence.

There must be a full range of responses to correspond to
the range of possible situations. Otherwise there is only the
all-or-nothing response, which is not a choice -- it is a
dilemma. The person who cannot cope with a mildly
threatening hostile act does nothing, or responds to the
mild threat as if it were a vicious assault. If the intended
victim is passive it encourages the assailant and assaultive
action is more likely to occur. Reacting to a mild threat as
though it were a vicious assault is inappropriate.

The objective of ethical self-defense instruction is to teach
appropriate and effective responses. The objective of this
book is to give information and guidance toward making
those appropriate responses.

### WHAT ARE NERVE CENTERS & PRESSURE POINTS?

"Nerve centers" and "pressure points" are not scientific
descriptions of anatomical entities. They are layman's
terms which we use for everyday discussion of this aspect
of our subject.

*Nerve center* is used to describe body areas which are most
susceptible to pain sensation on most people because of a
concentration of relatively exposed nerves. In this sense
the shin is a nerve center. Not all nerves are carriers of
impulses experienced as pain, so not all concentrations of
nerves produce a nerve center in our terms. The buttocks
have a high concentration of nerves, but this area is
ordinarily one of the least sensitive.

*Pressure point,* in this text, indicates an area which is
peculiarly vulnerable to injury or incapacitating pain.
An example is the windpipe.

SUPERSTITION OR KNOWLEDGE

The Asian fighting skills were practiced and developed many centuries prior to the discovery of the actual nature of vital body functions such as the process of digestion and the circulation of the blood.

Among the ancients, muscle contractions, palpitations, intestinal growling and other such internal stirrings and audible processes were thought to result from reptile spirits which resided within the body and that these hyperphysical serpents and dragons moved about in response to specific human activity.

We ought to be careful about accepting ancient ideas as truth merely because they are old. We may not have made much progress toward an understanding of the human psyche, but we do know a great deal more now than we used to know about our physical structure and our body functions.

If you are seriously interested in this subject field you should make a reasonably thorough study of anatomy and of the mechanics of the human body.

If you expect to be involved in self-defense instruction, even on an informal, nonprofessional club or group basis, you have an absolute responsibility to be informed. There are too many people in this field who are uninformed and who are circulating ancient superstitions and misconceptions. The only way to refute ignorance is with knowledge.

Take courses in anatomy and physiology, if you can. In many areas there are free adult education programs at the high school level. If you cannot take a formal class, use your local library for a self-directed study program using the reference books you will find there.

## KARATE, JUJITSU & ATEMI-WAZA

*Martial arts* is an omnibus term used to designate many
different styles of weaponless fighting as well as systems
of armed fighting. As the term is now used, it refers only
to those fighting styles which developed in Asian countries.
It would be more accurate to include among the martial
arts the skills which were originally used for combat
regardless of the country or region in which they were
developed. Fencing, wrestling, boxing and archery are
martial arts in exactly the same sense that judo, kendo,
karate, aikido and kung fu are martial arts.

There are literally hundreds of styles and substyles of the
weaponless martial arts but there is a relatively small group
of techniques utilized in all of them. The major groups of
techniques are: Grappling and bending and twisting the
joints (judo, aikido, wrestling); throwing and tripping and
takedowns (judo, wrestling); hand blows (boxing); hand
and foot blows (karate, jujitsu, kung fu, savate, atemi-
waza, Tai boxing).

Although there are many styles and substyles of karate
and kung fu, all of the styles utilize the techniques of
hitting and kicking at nerve centers and pressure points.
Although there are hundreds of styles of jujitsu, most of
them include techniques of hitting and kicking at nerve
centers and pressure points. Atemi-waza is solely con-
cerned with techniques of hitting and kicking at specific
nerve center and pressure point body targets.

The general term *martial arts* and the specialty terms such
as *karate, kung fu, judo, jujitsu, aikido* and other names
for the Asian-style fighting skills are used indiscriminately
by the lay public. For an overview of the subject field
and clarification of some of the differences and similarities
among the specialties see the current edition of the
*Encyclopedia Americana* which is available for reference
at most public libraries.

## COMPARISON of FIGHTING SYSTEMS

| | ATEMI-WAZA | BOXING | JUDO | JUJITSU | KARATE & KUNG FU | SAVATE | WRESTLING |
|---|---|---|---|---|---|---|---|
| Fist blows, blocks & parries | ★ | ★ | | ★ | ★ | ★ | |
| Open hand & arm blows | ★ | | | ★ | ★ | ★ | |
| High kicks | | | | ★ | ★ | ★ | |
| Low kicks | ★ | | | ★ | | ★ | |
| Holds, locks & grappling | | | ★ | ★ | | | ★ |
| Throws | | | ★ | ★ | | | |
| Takedowns | | | ★ | ★ | ★ | | ★ |
| Nerve centers & pressure points emphasized | ★ | | | ★ | ★ | | |
| Training emphasizes flexible response rather than rigid, prearranged actions | | ★ | ★ | | | ★ | ★ |

## PAIN & THE PSYCHODYNAMICS OF SELF-DEFENSE

For convenience we speak of pain as something which is
inflicted. In fact, pain is a more complicated matter.
Pain involves two factors--one is the application of a
stimulus and the other is the response to the stimulus.

There is an astonishing range of responses to exactly
the same stimulus. There are people who go to the
dentist calmly and are able to think about something
else while dental work is being done. Others go to the
dentist in a state of fearful agitation and endure dental
work in acute agony. There are individuals who can
present themselves for injections or innoculations with
no sign of anxiety. There are others who faint each time
they get a shot.

There are individuals whose fear and anxiety about
physical violence is so intense that the idea of the
possibility of assault is terrifying. For these people the
stimulus of a blow would probably provoke a very high
response of pain. Fearful, anxious individuals will
experience an assault with greater trauma than those who
have a higher tolerance for pain.

Just as different individuals respond differently to the
blows of an assault, different individuals will respond
in different ways to the blows of a physical defense action.

The basic concept in old-style self-defense  training is that
one must develop an extremely high level of fighting skill.
That concept derives from combat-oriented training. For
combat it is necessary to have the ability to win fights
and to have the capacity for inflicting maximum pain.

But pain is only one of the factors in self-defense. As
important as the ability to inflict pain is an understanding of the psychological interaction between the assailant
and the intended victim.

The relationships in self-defense are very different from
those in combat or in combat sports. It is a mistake to view

the three entirely different events as though they were
the same. In most sport contests it is not necessary to
inflict any pain in order to win. In battle it is necessary
to wound, incapacitate or kill the opponent in order to
win. The amount of pain necessary in practical self-
defense is only that which convinces the would-be
assailant that a spirited and orderly defense will be made
and that the intended victim will not be passive.

Effective self-defense, in many instances, does not even
involve inflicting pain or resorting to physical actions.
When physical actions are appropriate, they might
result in little pain, very great pain, or not pain at all!

Self-control, determined resistance, a refusal to accept the
role of victim are factors which could be much more
important for your safety and well-being than the ability
to inflict pain.

The person who chooses a helpless or seemingly vulnerable
individual as an object for physical violence is not brave.
In many instances of threatened assault the first indication
of refusal to be a passive victim is enough to deter the
assailant. This refusal might be verbal (no pain at all) or
it might, in the event of a serious assault, involve responding with a forceful blow.

The ability to refrain from using physical actions and the
ability to inflict appropriate pain are equally important.
It is not necessary to be a highly trained fighter in order
to present yourself as competent and self-reliant. Gesture,
attitude, language and tone can convey the message that
you refuse the role of passive victim. An assertive and
convincing manner of responding to the threat of assault
will reduce significantly the carrying out of the threat.

## THE MYTHS OF THE DEADLY BLOWS

Legend, fantasy, tall tales, movie and television fight
scenes  and ignorance have all contributed to the misconceptions and cult stories about the secret deadly
blows known only to an elect few of the masters of
the martial arts.

Among the myths, legends and misconceptions which
are solemnly repeated as though they were factual are
those of the master who could reach in with his dagger
hand and pluck out a still-beating heart, or pull the spine
out of the living body of his adversary.  There is the tale
of the death without contact and the terrible and
mysterious seven-year death.  One of the most widely
circulated misconceptions is that a blow upward under
the nose can cause death by driving the nasal bones into
the brain.

### CAN NASAL BONES BE DRIVEN INTO THE BRAIN?

This piece of nonsense can be disproved by looking at the
human skull structure in an anatomy book, or by examin-
ing a skull in an anatomy class.

*Any* sufficiently powerful blow to the head could be fatal.
But the cause of death from a forceful blow up under the
nose would not be related to nasal bones driven into the
brain.  Fatality would result from shock transmitted to the
brain.

Most of the nose is not bone but cartilage.  The bones of
the nose are more fragile than the surrounding skull
structure.  A forceful blow would fracture the nasal bones
more easily than it would fracture the skull.  Even if the
nasal bones were intact there is no channel through which
they could enter the brain.  The only entrances to the brain
from the angle of an upward blow are the passages for
nerves and blood vessels and they are much too small to
accommodate nasal bones.

So while it is possible to deliver a fatal blow by striking up
under the nose, death would not result from bones entering
the brain but from concussion or ruptured blood vessels.

## PLUCKING OUT THE HEART OR SPINE

Every culture has its suprahuman heroes, demi-gods and legendary figures. Myth is part of all cultures and it serves a serious purpose -- part poetic, part prophetic. Myths create an orderly past and give us a sense of a future in which we are greater than we can ever be today.

There is a danger in regarding legend as literal truth. If you believe everything -- without verification -- it will dull your ability to distinguish fantasy from fact, lies from truth. A credulous person - one who does not ask questions and demand verifiable proof -- is in a perilous position. As a consumer, as a voter, as a participant in a highly complex society, it is your duty and in your survival interest to be able to tell the difference between fantasy and reality, between promotional hucksterism and plain fact.

So, if you approach the tales of the karate masters as wonderful Asian folklore - fine! The problem is that too many people believe that they are factual.

The chilling tale of the karate master with the power to reach into a human body and pluck out the heart or spine can only be taken as legend. It is patently absurd to think of proving or disproving it. Better to leave it where it belongs, along with the exploits of Paul Bunyan and John Henry.

## TOUCH-OF-DEATH

The touch-of-death story is clearly a tale of magic. The possessor of this mysterious power to cause death by merely touching at a secret spot has never been seen nor has any victim ever been identified. This is a great story for entertainment-by-fright.

A variation of the touch-of-death legend is the seven-year death. In this version the master possesses the power to touch or to strike at an adversary so that death occurs seven years later.

It is conceivable that in a fight there could be internal injury leading to deterioration or malfunction of a vital organ and that death could follow after an interval. That would be an accident. But the seven-year death tale does not assign the possibility of accident. What it proposes is that someone with secret powers could predetermine the exact degree of injury, deliver exactly the right amount of force at precisely the spot to cause a lingering death at a specified future time. There is no acceptable proof of such a possibility.

There is no secret to it. Anyone who can deliver a forceful blow of any style to a vulnerable part of the body is capable of delivering a "deadly" blow. A boxing blow of sufficient force is as deadly as a karate or kung fu blow of equal force.

## THE MEDIA

Entertainment movies and television shows do not make claims to educate us. Neither do the gossip "news about people" publications. But most of us still have the belief that we can trust what we see in the newspapers. Careful! The news media is quick to report as "news" an event that is out of the ordinary. They do not always verify their information.

The widely reported story of a man rendered unconscious by pressure applied into his armpits (by a woman he was attempting to assault) was hailed as a new and wonderful technique of self-defense. Nonsense.

Individuals who are assaultive are not in control of their emotions and are in a state of high anxiety. Breakdown, weeping, and running away are not uncommon reactions among assailants confronted with resistant behavior. The most likely explanation for the man's unconscious state is that he fainted.

## HAND CONDITIONING IS NOT NECESSARY!

Hand conditioning, the hardening and callusing of the hands, is not appropriate for sport or self-defense karate or jujitsu; it is irrelevant to judo.

In sport karate, players do not make contact or they wear gloves.

In contest  where contact is prohibited by the rules, players who have conditioned hands are required to wear bandages to minimize the possibility of injury if accidental contact is made.

In matches where contact is permitted, the players use padded gloves.  A karate contestant who had spent years in hand conditioning would not be allowed to hit the opponent player with his hand weapon.

Sport judo rules forbid striking the opponent player with hand or foot blows.

For practical self-defense it is neither desirable nor necessary to condition your hands.  Hand conditioning was an appropriate feature of ancient karate training. Because it was sometimes necessary to break through the wooden armor of the Samurai soldier, karate fighters in feudal times were required to spend years of effort to callus and desensitize their hands and feet so that they could deliver forceful blows to hard surfaces without feeling pain.

Today there is no reason to strike at hard surfaces in a manner which would hurt your normal, unconditioned hand.  With an understanding of appropriate body target areas, you can avoid striking at hard, bony areas such as the collarbone (clavicle).  When you do strike at a bony structure, such as the knee or the bridge of the nose, you can hit with appropriately forceful blows without hurting yourself.  A kick into the knee does not require conditioning; hitting with the side of the closed fist onto the nose delivers enough force for self-defense use.

Heavy conditioning can cause permanent injury to your hands and it can seriously impair manual dexterity. Extreme hand conditioning is irreversible. The ability to do skillful, intricate work might be seriously reduced. If a job requires contact with the public, the misshapen appearance of conditioned hands could be an impediment to employment.

Heavy conditioning implies willingness to fight. Should you need to defend yourself on the street, you might have difficulty persuading the law that you were defending yourself; the evidence of conditioned hands would suggest preparation for fighting.

Hand conditioning is necessary if you want to do stunts and tricks such as breaking bricks without hurting yourself. If you really feel that it is important to show off in such a manner, you will have to work at long-term hand conditioning. Be aware that once you have heavily conditioned hands, you are risking the chance that they will never again be normal. It is a heavy price to pay for doing a stunt.

## ACCURACY OF THE DESCRIPTIONS

It is my objective to be as accurate as possible in describing the effects of blows and techniques commonly used in self-defense and in sport fighting. There is a difference between accuracy for this purpose and exactness in the scientific sense.

To make a scientific evaluation of the effect and consequences of any particular technique (a hand blow, for example) it would be necessary to have the following information:

a. A precise measurement of the force of the blow.

b. An exact description of the area struck.

c. An exact measurement of the angle at which the blow was struck.

d. A complete description of the general health, past medical history and body structure of the person struck.

e. Professional medical examination of any injury, or, in the event of death, post-mortem examination and report.

f. To measure pain and emotional trauma one would have to know the state of mind and the general pain tolerance of the person struck.

It is clear that all of these complex factors cannot be examined to yield the information we want for our present purpose. Instead we must rely on the best available sources which come close to and are relevant to the subject. (In Nazi Germany doctors did pain-tolerance and injury experiments on healthy human beings. It is to be hoped that we will never see a repetition of this kind of "science.")

In the interest of achieving the degree of accuracy which is appropriate for this book there is frequent use of the words "possible" and "probable." They are used to remind you that exactness is not implied. "Possible" indicates that there is a chance the effect of the blow would produce the results described; "probable" indicates that there is a reasonable expectation that the blow would produce the results described.

The health and emotional state of the person being struck would modify the effect of the blow. The degree of force would modify the effect of a blow. The relative sizes of the people involved would be a modifying factor. For example, it is likely that a hand blow struck straight in at the solar plexus of a large person would yield the result of little pain and no other effect, but it would be inaccurate to say that such a result could be expected *under any circumstances.* If the large person being struck had an internal abnormality, weakness or disease and the person striking the blow had practiced to develop a fast punch which could deliver considerable force, the result could be serious.

COMPARING THE EFFECTS OF BLOWS

In considering the probable or possible effects of any particular blow, there are three situations to be considered: The opponents could be of approximately equal size and strength; the blow could be struck by a larger, stronger person against a smaller, slighter person; the blow could be used to defend against a larger, heavier assailant. There could be dramatic differences of effect in these different situations. Some examples follow.

1,2,3. In the three photos the identical open-hand slash is used and it is delivered to the identical target-- onto the bridge of the nose.

1. The two people shown are about equal in size and build. The probable effects of this blow would be pain, possible bleeding and disorientation. Blurred vision might result temporarily. Permanent or serious injury is unlikely.

2. When the identical blow is delivered by a larger, heavier person against a smaller, lighter individual there is a greater possibility of serious or permanent injury. Because of the more favorable angle at which the blow is delivered to the target, because of the greater force delivered to the target and because of the presumably greater vulnerability of the person being struck, all of the effects described for photo 1 are present, but to a considerably greater degree. In addition there is a possibility of breaking the nasal bone and even the possibility of brain damage. Brain damage would not result from fracture of the nasal bone but from shock force of a blow to the head. A sufficiently forceful blow to any part of the head could cause brain damage.

3. A smaller, slighter person strikes the identical blow at a larger, heavier individual. The blow is the same as that shown in photos 1 and 2, but the small person hits at an awkward angle and would have difficulty reaching the target in the relationship illustrated here.

The probable effects of a full force blow in this instance would be quite different from the probable effects of the same blow illustrated in photo 2. Some pain might result but the likelihood of injury is remote.

1

2

3

4,5,6. In these photos the variants of size relationship, strength and the angle of the blow are shown for an open-hand slash into the side of the neck.

4. When opponents are of equal size and build the edge-of-hand blow struck into the side of the neck might stun and disorient. Depending on the force of the blow, there is a possibility of numbing the arm. A sufficiently forceful blow could cause unconsciousness and possible convulsions.

5. When the same blow is delivered at a smaller person by a larger adversary, there is greater probability of unconsciousness resulting. A sufficiently powerful blow could transmit shock force via the neck bones to result in brain damage and there is a possibility of irreversible damage to the carotid artery.

6. A forceful blow struck by the smaller individual against a heavier, stronger, larger adversary would result in pain and possible disorientation. The probability of injury is remote.

WEAPONS

The possible and probable effects of blows as they are described in this text refer to weaponless hand and foot blows. If a stick, bludgeon, baton, or any other weapon or implement were used the effects of the blow would be radically different. There would be a considerable increase in the degree of pain, the likelihood of injury, the seriousness of the injury and (if the blow were struck at a vulnerable area) a higher risk of fatality.

4

5

6

**7,8,9.** A knuckle blow is delivered to the solar plexus in three different situations.

**7.** As shown here with equal opponents, the probable effects would be pain, disorientation and gasping for breath.

**8.** Delivered at the angle shown and in the relationship of size and build illustrated, the probability of injury is dramatically increased. There could be referral shock to the spleen and to other vital internal organs.

**9.** When used by a smaller, slighter person against a heavier, stronger person, the identical blow has little effect.

7

8

9

10,11,12. Practical self-defense techniques are those which depend to the *least* degree upon relative power, size and build. Kicking into the knee or shin is an example of a highly practical self-defense action.

Though the effect would be different in different size relationships, the major advantage of this kick is shown in all three photos: The person kicking at the assailant does not have to come within fist or hand range of the assailant.

10. An adversary of approximately equal size is vulnerable to a kick into the knee or shin.

11. Kicking against a smaller person involves a considerably greater possibility of inflicting injury.

12. Although the probability of injury is considerably less when the same kick is delivered by a small person against a larger adversary, it is an effective technique for practical self-defense.

10

11

12

In contrast to the kick into the knee or shin, which can be effective for small or large people, the tactic shown in 13, 14 and 15 is virtually useless for a small person and is a high-risk-of-injury blow if applied by a strong, large person against someone slight or frail.

13. The fist or open-hand blow to the base of the neck could cause considerable pain if applied to an individual of approximately equal size and build. There is a possibility, though not great likelihood, of dislocating the seventh cervical vertebra, which is a serious injury.

14. The identical blow struck with force by a larger, stronger person against a smaller individual involves the probability of serious permanent injury.

15. Used by a small person against a larger assailant, it is unlikely that enough pain would result to make this action practical for self-defense.

## MOVIE & TV FIGHT SCENES

Before the "karate or kung fu killer" had been discovered by filmmakers, it was the little judo expert who would creep up and drop the big guy with a judo chop to the back of the neck.   It always worked in the movies because there was a stunt man paid to fall down. We rather suspected that was the case. Nowadays there are some actors who are highly skilled in the martial arts  or  who take special training for a fight scene, which makes it very difficult for the audience to distinguish reality from make-believe.

But no filmed fight scene is real regardless of the actor's fighting skill. Filmed fight scenes follow a written script which determines who shall win and who shall lose. The scene is choreographed and rehearsed over and over. It is shot many times to get the most dramatic effect. Sound effects, trampolines, stunt men reacting, special visual effects and camera angles--these and other film techniques are used to produce a spectacular fight scene.

— ALICE McGRATH

13

14

15

# NERVE CENTERS & PRESSURE POINTS

TEMPLE AREA. 16.

It is widely believed that the temple area is extremely vulnerable because of a mistaken notion that the skull is thinner and more fragile in this region. An examination of a skull in an anatomy class or in an anatomy textbook will confirm that the bone is as thick at the temple area as it is at several other places on the skull.

Vulnerability in the temple area is associated with the shape of the bone rather than its thickness. Because the skull is flat at the temple area referral shock to the brain is more intense than the referral shock of a blow to a curved skull area. If sufficient *force* is delivered, any type of blow to the temple area or any other part of the head could be fatal without fracturing the skull. Hemorrhage of blood vessels of the brain is the most common cause of death following a forceful blow to the head.

† Equal adversary: A moderate blow startles and stuns, and causes pain. With repeated blows to the head there is increased possibility of injury such as is sustained by some boxers whom we call "punch drunk." As noted above, any blow to the head, if sufficiently forceful, involves probability of brain injury.

† Against a smaller person: A moderate or heavy blow could result in unconsciousness or convulsions and there is the possibility of irreversible brain damage.

† Against a larger assailant: A moderate blow can startle and distract. A heavy blow could stun. Unless the larger assailant were peculiarly vulnerable, it is not likely that a small person would cause serious injury.

Blows which can be used are the heel-of-palm blow, the slash and the hammer blow. If an assailant is behind you, an elbow blow or slash can be used.

Looking down onto a skull section. Compare the bone structure at the temple area (frontal bone) with the thickness of the skull at other areas.

FRONTAL BONE

Ethmoid bone

Orbital plate

Sphenoid bone

Lesser wing

Mandible

Jugum

Greater wing

Body

Basilar part

Foramen magnum

Condylar part

Squamous part

Parietal bone

Parietal bone

Occipital bone

ONTO THE NOSE.  17.

If you are already in close to an assailant, this is an excellent target.  DO NOT step in close to hit at the nose
if you are out of fist-hitting range!

Hitting onto the nose is very likely to hurt, confuse and
disorient an assailant.  Drawing the head back and water-
ing of the eyes are the two most common reactions to
being hit on the nose.  Even a moderate blow results in
considerable pain.  A bloody nose, while not serious,
has a positive psychological effect in self-defense.
Even when other possible targets are protected by
clothing, an assailant's nose is almost always presented
as an easy target.

† Equal adversary: A moderate blow startles and stuns;
there is considerable pain; bleeding might result.  A
heavy blow could separate cartilage from the bone.

† Against a smaller person: A moderate blow causes
considerable pain and disorientation.  A forceful blow
could result in separation of cartilage from the bone
and could fracture the nasal bone.

† Against a larger assailant: A moderate blow causes pain.
A heavy blow causes considerable pain and perhaps
bleeding.

The most efficient hand blows onto the top of the nose
are the hammer blow* and the edge-of-hand blow (also
called slash, chop or knife-hand blow).

* The hammer blow is a closed-hand pounding action
hitting with the edge of the curled hand.

An open-hand slash onto the nose.

A closed-hand hammer blow onto the nose.

SIDE OF THE NOSE. 18.

Striking into the side of the nose is practical if the
assailant is behind you.

† Equal adversary: A light blow distracts and usually
results in a reflex action of pulling the head back. A
moderate blow causes pain, might cause bleeding and
there is a possibility of dislodging cartilage. A heavy
blow would involve a possibility of nasal bone fracture
in addition to the other effects just described.

† Against a smaller person: With a moderate or heavy
blow there is considerable pain and disorientation, bleeding
and the likelihood of dislocation of cartilage and/or bone
fracture.

† Against a larger assailant: Striking into the side of the
nose is distracting and there is momentary disorientation.
A heavy blow could also cause bleeding and there is a
possibility of cartilage separating from the bone. There
is little likelihood of serious injury.

UP UNDER THE NOSE.  19.

This is an excellent target for a smaller person against a larger assailant, close in.  Although it is widely believed that hitting up under the nose is a "deadly" blow, it is actually a low-risk-of-injury tactic.

† Equal adversary: A moderate blow causes pain and distraction; bleeding might result.  A heavy blow might fracture the maxillary bone and/or cause cartilage separation from the bone.

† Against a smaller person: A moderate blow could cause bleeding and possible cartilage separation from the bone.  A heavy blow could fracture the maxillary bone.

† Against a larger assailant: A moderate blow causes pain and momentary distraction.  A heavy blow could cause bleeding.  The likelihood of serious injury is remote.

From the front, the most effective blows up under the nose are the heel-of-palm blow or the slash.  A slash can be used against an assailant from the rear; an elbow blow is effective, but requires greater precision than a slash blow.

An open-hand slash up under the nose.

EYES. 20.

Striking into the eyes is a very high-risk-of-injury
tactic. Its use would be justified only in the most serious
kinds of assault. If your life is threatened, or extreme
bodily harm is intended and if you are already close in
there might be no practical alternative.

The slightest contact blow or fingernail scratch could
result in serious and permanent eye injury. There is no
justification for striking into the eyes if any other defense
action would be effective. In some styles of kung fu
training there is heavy emphasis on clawing and poking
into the eyes. Such instruction is dangerously out of
date; it does not take into consideration the legal, social
or emotional consequences of inappropriately punitive
responses to non-life-threatening assault.

† Because of the extreme delicacy and vulnerability of
the eye, there is scarcely any difference in the effects
of blows struck by a large or small person. Poking,
clawing or stabbing into the eyes can cause permanent
injury resulting in sight impairment or blindness.

UP UNDER THE CHIN. 21.

This is an excellent target for practical defense and it is easily available to a smaller person already close in to a larger assailant.

† Equal adversary: A moderate blow snaps the head back and puts the assailant in an off balance position. A heavy blow could knock him unconscious. This is a classic boxer's knockout blow.

† Against a smaller person: A moderate blow could put him off balance, cause pain and jar the head. A heavy blow could result in unconsciousness. There is a possibility of bone or tooth injury.

† Against a larger assailant: A moderate blow jars the head and snaps it back. A heavy blow could put him off balance.

The heel-of-palm blow up under the chin can be used as a standing technique or from a seated position.

AT THE EAR. 22.

Blows to the ears are taught in many old-style martial
arts. My objection to this target for modern self-defense
is that it is not a practical striking area for a smaller person
against a larger assailant and if it is used against a smaller
person there is a possibility of hearing impairment.

†Equal adversary: A moderate blow can cause pain. A
heavy blow might injure the inner ear.

† Against a smaller person: A moderate blow can jar the
head and cause pain. A sufficiently forceful blow could
cause hearing impairment or brain injury.

† Against a larger assailant: A moderate blow is not
likely to be effective. A vigorous, cupped-hand blow
could cause pain.

UP UNDER THE EAR. 23.

The hollow behind the ear is an area to which pressure can
be applied to effect pain by grinding with the thumb or
knuckle.

WINDPIPE/ADAM'S APPLE.  24.

Unless threatened with great bodily harm or vicious
assault, striking into any portion of the windpipe (trachea)
or onto the Adam's apple (thryoid cartilage) is neither
justified nor appropriate.     The area at the front of the
throat is a most vulnerable, high-risk-of-injury  target  and
should be avoided unless  there is no practical available
alternative.

† Equal adversary: Striking straight in with a moderate
blow would result in pain, gasping and choking.  There is
a possibility of fatal injury.

† Against a smaller person: A moderate blow involves
possibility of fatal injury; a heavy blow dramatically increases the likelihood of fatal injury.

† Against a larger assailant: A moderate blow could
result in gasping and choking.  A heavy blow could be
fatal.

Against a vicious assault, and if you are already close in
to the assailant, an edge-of-hand slash or a forearm blow
could be used.

*PRESSURE*  against any part of the windpipe (trachea)
also involves risk of injury.  Very slight pressure can cause
pain.   Heavy pressure against the trachea involves a high
probability of fatality which could result from rupture of
the trachea or from strangulation.

A person against whom a trachea pressure technique  is
applied is likely to struggle forward against the hold, thus
increasing the force of the pressure.  It is almost impossible
for the person applying the hold to regulate the degree of
pressure.

## UP UNDER THE JAW.  25.

In this area there is a concentration of nerves.  The target
is behind and up under the jawbone.  Except for the in-
tensity of pain, there is no appreciable difference if this
is done by a larger or smaller person.  A jabbing or poking
blow results in considerable pain.  The extended knuckle
or fingertips can be used.

## THROAT HOLLOW.  26.

Below the thyroid cartilage there is a hollow where the
windpipe (trachea) is least protected and most exposed.
*Slight* pressure at the trachea in this area can be used to
push an assailant away.  Forceful blows into the throat
hollow involve a high risk of serious injury.

Because of the vulnerability of the trachea, the result of
light pressure against it will be much the same if done by a
smaller or a larger person.  Control of someone who is
annoying or offensive but is not threatening great harm
can be effected by placing the thumb into the hollow and
applying slight pressure.  Heavy pressure would involve
probability of serious injury or fatality.  Forceful
knuckle jabs or finger stabs would have the same effect
as striking into the thyroid cartilage.

Forceful blows, heavy pressure or vigorous stabbing into
the throat hollow would be appropriate and justified
only if great bodily harm were threatened.

Slight fingertip pressure into
the throat hollow.

SIDE OF THE NECK.  27.

This area includes the carotid artery and the jugular
vein, and is an excellent practical self-defense target.  It
is sensitive to pain but it is not a high-risk-of-injury
target unless a very forceful blow is struck or unless the
person struck is particularly vulnerable--frail or ill.

† Equal adversary: A moderately forceful blow causes
pain.  A vigorous blow could cause temporary stunning.
A very heavy blow could result in unconsciousness.

† Against a smaller person: A moderate blow could cause
stunning.  A heavy blow could result in unconsciousness
and a very forceful blow involves the possibility of fatal
injury.

† Against a larger assailant: A moderate blow causes
pain.  A forceful blow causes considerable pain and
disorientation.  It is not likely that a small person
striking against a larger assailant could deliver sufficient
force to result in injury.

The open-hand slash is the most efficient blow against
the side of the neck.

*PRESSURE* against the side of the neck (a hold or bar
at the carotid artery/jugular vein area) is considerably
less likely to injure than a hold or bar applied against
the trachea.  Even when the pressure against the side of
the neck is sufficient to render someone unconscious, it
is not probable that it would result in irreparable or
fatal injury.

This is not a practical self-defense technique for the lay
citizen, but it is an excellent control tactic for professionals who have been properly trained in its appropriate use.

A slash into the side of the neck, delivered with the palm up.

A control hold applied against the side of the neck -- at the carotid artery.

There is a high risk of injury --*including fatal injury*-- if pressure is applied against the front of the throat at the thyroid cartilage and windpipe.

MUSCLE AT THE BASE OF THE NECK.  28.

Where the neck and shoulder join there is a muscle area
which can present a practical self-defense target.

† Equal adversary: Striking down onto the muscle with
a moderate blow causes pain.  A forceful blow could numb
the arm for a short time and it might result in muscle
spasm, immobilizing the arm.

† Against a smaller person: A moderate blow causes
considerable pain and could numb the arm.  A forceful
blow could result in a longer period of immobility and
there is a possibility of muscle injury.

† Against a larger assailant: A moderate blow is ineffective.
A forceful blow causes pain and could briefly incapacitate
the arm.

The most practical blow is an open-hand slash.


COLLARBONE.  29.

This high ridge of bone is a favored target in old-style
martial arts.  Although fracturing the collarbone
(clavicle) may be a disabling tactic which would be
appropriate against a serious assault, I do not favor it
for modern self-defense because it is hardly possible
except for a larger person against a smaller individual
or for those who have had considerable training and
hand conditioning.

† Equal adversary:  A moderate blow is ineffective.  A
forceful hammer blow could fracture the clavicle.

† Against a smaller person: A moderate blow is painful
and jarring.  A forceful hammer blow involves  probability of fracture.

† Against a larger assailant:  Little likelihood of appreciable effect.

A slash down onto the
muscle at the base of
the neck.

## BASE OF THE SKULL. 30.

At the base of the skull is a target area of very limited use. Consisting of the first cervical vertebra and the second cervical vertebra, it is not practical for smaller individuals against a larger assailant as shown in photo 15. It is also a high-risk-of-injury target if used against a frail or small person by a powerful individual.

† Equal adversary: A moderate blow causes pain and possible headache. A sufficiently forceful blow could be fatal for one of two reasons: An extremely forceful blow directed upward against the target could refer fatal shock to the brain. Directed straight in at the target, a powerful blow could dislodge the first vertebra (the atlas) or fracture the second vertebra (the axis), either of which might result in permanent paralysis or fatality because of injury to the spinal cord.

† Against a smaller person: The probability of paralysis or fatality is increased if a power blow is directed against someone small or frail.

† Against a larger assailant: A moderate blow is ineffective. A forceful blow could cause pain or headache.

## BASE OF THE NECK. 31.

A cliche of movie and television fight scenes is the judo chop, karate chop or rabbit punch to the base of the neck (seventh cervical vertebra). In films, the adversary goes down, no matter how big he is. In real life this does not happen.

For street defense this is not an appropriate target. A smaller person cannot use it effectively; if a larger individual strikes a power blow against a smaller person there is a high risk of injury.

To locate the target on your own self, drop your head forward and you can feel the prominent bone at the base of the back of your neck which is the seventh cervical vertebra.

† Equal adversary: A moderate blow jars the body and
causes pain. A forceful blow causes considerable pain
and if it is sufficiently forceful there is a possibility of
serious injury, paralysis or fatality.

† Against a smaller person: There is higher probability
of serious injury, paralysis or fatality when a power blow
is struck against a small or frail individual. Because of
the angle at which a larger person is likely to strike at
a smaller person, referral shock to the aortic arch is a
possibility. The aortic arch is the major pathway for
blood supply to the upper and lower parts of the body.
If there is injury to the aortic arch, internal bleeding
results and death is highly probable.

† Against a larger adversary: A moderate blow is ineffective. A forceful blow could cause pain.

BETWEEN THE SHOULDER BLADES. 32.

Slightly above and between the prominent bones of the
shoulder blades is an area which is struck with the in-
tention of referring shock force into the heart or the
aortic arch and the vagus nerve. I do not favor this as
a practical self-defense target. It is either high-risk (when
a power blow is applied) or it is ineffectual, depending on
the relative size and frame of the persons involved.

† Equal adversary: A moderate blow causes pain. A
heavy blow could refer shock force into vital organs
with a possibility of serious injury.

† Against a smaller person: The probability of serious
internal injury increases with the force of the blow.
Against a frail or slight individual this is a high-risk-of-
injury area.

† Against a larger assailant: A moderate blow is ineffectual. A forceful blow could cause pain. Against a larger,
heavier assailant the purpose of striking into this area
would not be to effect pain but perhaps to push him off
balance.

KIDNEY AREA.  33.

The kidneys are located at about the waist level, a few
inches on either side of the spine.  Approximately half
of the kidney is protected by the lower ribs; the lower
half is relatively unprotected, vulnerable and sensitive.
If a power blow is delivered by a strong person there is
high risk of serious internal injury.

† Equal adversary: A moderate hand blow is painful;
there is slight possibility of internal injury.  A heavy blow
into the kidney area causes considerable pain and there
is probability of internal injury.  A sufficiently forceful
blow could be fatal.

† Against a smaller person: Striking into the kidney area
of a smaller person involves a risk of internal injury.  The
probability of delivering a fatal blow increases with the
force of the blow and the relative sizes of the persons
involved.

† Against a larger assailant: A moderate hand blow is
unlikely to have an appreciable effect.  A forceful hand
blow could cause pain.

A hammer blow or elbow blow is used to strike into
this area.  In karate training, kicking into this area is
commonly taught as a self-defense tactic.  I do not
favor this because of the high level of skill required
and because the risk of injury from a kick is considerably more than from a hand blow.

† There is also a possibility of injury to the kidney by
striking a forceful blow into the side; if the last rib is
struck with sufficient force there is a possibility of a
fractured rib rupturing the kidney.

## SOLAR PLEXUS. 34.

This is not an anatomic entity, but is a term used to describe a striking area. It is the region below the breast bone, where the ribs part. There is a critical difference in the degree of pain, risk of injury and other effects depending on the angle of delivery of the blow as well as on the force of the blow and the health and frame of the individual being struck.

† Equal adversary: A moderate blow causes pain and could result in what is commonly called "knocking the wind out" which is in fact a temporary stoppage of breathing resulting from striking the diaphragm. A forceful blow could result in internal injury to the vital organs. A moderate blow struck in an upward direction causes considerable pain and sends referred shock to the vital organs with some possibility of internal injury. A forceful blow struck in an upward direction could cause serious permanent injury to one or more of the vital organs and there is a possibility of fatality.

† Against a smaller person: A straight-in moderate blow can interfere with breathing, is very painful and could stun. A forceful straight-in blow could result in unconsciousness and there is a probability of internal injury. A moderate blow struck in an upward direction involves possibility of internal injury. A heavy upward blow is a high-risk-of-injury tactic and the danger of fatality is increased by the force of the blow and the physical and emotional state of the person being struck.

† Against a larger adversary: Struck in an upward direction, a moderate hand blow can cause pain; a forceful hand blow could cause considerable pain and might briefly affect breathing. Unless the person being struck were particularly vulnerable because of illness or impairment, there is little likelihood that injury would result.

Straight-in blows are delivered with the fist or extended knuckle. An upward blow is delivered with the heel-of-palm or extended-knuckle blow. An elbow blow can be used to strike into the solar plexus region against an assailant standing behind you. A kick into the solar plexus delivers greater force than a forceful hand blow and because of the angle of delivery is more likely to cause severe injury.

An upward blow (left) delivers far greater shock force to the internal organs than does a straight-in blow (right).

SIDE OF BODY, UNDER LAST RIB. 35.

This area is sensitive in a special way. Most people are
ticklish here, but it is also easy to cause pain by jabbing
directly below the last rib.

† Equal adversary: Digging with the extended knuckle
or striking an open-hand blow would cause pain.

† Against a smaller person: A grinding action with the
extended knuckle causes considerable pain with hardly
any possibility of internal injury. A forceful hand blow
or a kick might result in internal injury; if the last rib
is struck with sufficient force it can fracture and might
rupture the kidney--a very serious injury.

† Against a larger assailant: A digging action with an
extended knuckle could be used to effect release from the
grip of a larger person who is not threatening serious
assault. It is unlikely that a smaller person could use a
hand blow to this area with appreciable effect.

Digging into the side with knuckle
extended -- it is a grinding action.

INSIDE OF ELBOW JOINT. 36.

Striking into the bend of the elbow causes pain and it
bends the arm.  This is a good striking point for practical
self-defense; the smaller person need not come within
the hitting range of the assailant in order to hit the target.

† Equal adversary: A moderate blow causes pain; a
moderately forceful blow will bend the arm (or arms--
simultaneous blows can be struck).  A forceful blow will
bend the arm and there can be a numbing effect which
persists for a brief time.  The numbing effect is similar
to that which occurs when you hit the nerve at the back
of the elbow joint (the funny bone).

† Against a smaller person: A moderate blow causes pain
and can bend the arm (or arms).  A forceful blow causes
considerable pain, bends the arm and could result in numbness lasting from a few moments to as much as several
hours, during which time the arm is completely or
partially incapacitated.

† Against a larger assailant: A heavy blow into the elbow
could bend the arm and cause pain.

The open-hand slash is the most effective hand blow
into the bend of the elbow.  A hammer blow could also
be used.

OUTSIDE OF ELBOW JOINT. 37.

There is limited practical value to the tactic of striking at
the back of the elbow joint.  In some circumstances, the
arm may be extended in such a way that the back of the
elbow presents itself as a target.  It can be struck to
effect pain or it can be struck with force to incapacitate
the arm.

† Equal adversary: A moderate blow causes pain. A forceful blow could cause extreme hyperextension and could injure or tear cartilage, incapacitating the arm. Surgery is required to restore cartilage and muscle function unless the injury is slight.

† Against a smaller person: The probability of injury to muscle and cartilage increases dramatically when a forceful blow is applied against a smaller person. Moderate pressure against the elbow joint to hyperextend it might be a suitable control tactic for a law enforcement officer.

† Against a larger assailant: A moderate blow would have little appreciable effect. A forceful blow could cause pain and might numb the arm briefly.

A forearm blow is most efficient. A hammer blow could be used but would require greater precision.

FOREARM MOUND.  38.

Just beyond the elbow is an area which, on most people, is very sensitive to pain.  If you extend your arm you can see the top of the mound, which is the target area.  Using a hand blow onto the forearm mound, it is not necessary to hit with precision.  A blow aimed at the mound will refer force into the sensitive area.  If you press your thumb into your own arm at this point you will discover how little pressure is needed to effect pain.

† Equal adversary: A moderate blow causes pain.  A forceful blow causes considerable pain and can numb the arm.

† Against a smaller person: A moderate blow causes considerable pain and possible numbness.  A forceful blow can numb and partially incapacitate the arm for from a few minutes to as much as an hour.

† Against a larger assailant: A moderate blow causes slight pain and distraction.  A forceful blow causes considerable pain and can numb the arm briefly.

The most effective blow is the open-hand slash.

An open-hand slash is used to hit the forearm mound.

WRIST. 39.

Striking at the wrist is principally used as a deflecting action. Although a smaller person cannot easily block a larger assailant's arm, hitting the wrist with a sharp, slashing blow can deflect a reaching or grabbing attempt.

† Equal adversary: Deflection.

† Against a smaller person: A heavy blow could cause bone injury.

† Against a larger assailant: Deflection.

40, 41. The forearm mound and the wrist can also be target areas from the rear.

BACK OF UPPER ARM. 42.

At the back of the arm, midway between the elbow and shoulder, is a sensitive area.

† Equal adversary: A moderate blow has little effect. A forceful blow causes pain and possible numbness.

† Against a smaller person: A moderate blow causes pain and could numb the arm. A forceful blow causes considerable pain and could cause muscle spasm.

† Against a larger adversary. A heavy blow would cause some pain, but this is not a particularly good target for a smaller person against a larger assailant.

LOWER FOREARM.  43.

About two inches above the wrist on the thumb side of
the forearm there is a sensitive area.

† Equal adversary: A moderate blow is somewhat painful.  A forceful blow causes considerable pain.

† Against a smaller person: A moderate blow is painful.  A forceful blow causes considerable pain and might
result in a bone bruise.

† Against a larger assailant: A moderate blow is ineffectual.  A forceful blow is painful.

The open-hand slash or forearm block, blow or parry can
be used against the sensitive area to deflect and to cause
distracting pain.  Or, as shown below, the outer forearm
can be the target for a deflecting action.

A forearm block  against the forearm.

BACK OF THE HAND.  44.

The back of the hand is sensitive between the tendons and bones.  A grinding or digging action is used.

† Regardless of the relative size of the people, digging into the back of the hand with an extended knuckle is likely to be quite painful.

LOWER ABDOMINAL AREA. 45.

As has been noted repeatedly, the effect of any blow is
modified by the factors of force delivered to the target
area, general health and build of the person being struck,
the angle at which the blow is delivered and the emotional
and physical stance of the person being hit. These complex factors are particularly critical with respect to a
blow into the lower abdomen (pelvic region). From the
front, the bladder and lower intestines are unprotected
by bony structure; in women the reproductive organs
are vulnerable.

I view this as an inappropriate target for general self-
defense. The degree of force necessary to effect pain
carries with it a high risk of injury to vital organs.

A smaller person cannot strike into this area with much
likelihood of appreciable effect unless the smaller individual is highly trained and can deliver a powerful
blow.

† Equal adversary: A moderate hand blow causes pain.
A forceful blow causes considerable pain and there is
a possibility of internal injury.

† Against a smaller person: A moderate blow is painful
and might cause internal injury. With a forceful blow
there is considerable risk of injury to the internal organs.

† Against a larger assailant: A moderate hand blow is
unlikely to produce appreciable effect. A forceful blow
could cause considerable pain. There is a possibility of
injury if a kick is used.

GROIN. 46.

Although hitting and kicking into the groin is a classic
technique of old-style self-defense and grabbing the
testicles is often taught for women's self-defense, I
do not favor this area as a target. A blow or kick into
the groin is excruciatingly painful, but it is an almost
automatic reaction for men to protect the groin.

In many instances of assault the groin is not available
as a target area. It is necessary to come in very close in
order to use a knee kick to the groin; unless you are
already in close, it is unwise to move into hitting distance.
There is a strong element of sexual counterviolence in the
use of this tactic and many people are reluctant to use it
for this reason.

Violent, assaultive individuals and punitive persons are
likely to recommend groin blows even when less repug-
nant defense tactics would be effective and appropriate.

In those situations in which a blow to the groin would be
appropriate, a knee kick is used close in. Where an
extended-leg (ball of foot or stamping) kick could be
used, I would strongly recommend the knee as an alternative target.

UPPER INNER THIGH. 47.

Along the inner thigh, extending about halfway down to the knee, there is a very sensitive area.

† Equal adversary: A moderate, penetrating blow causes pain. A forceful blow causes considerable pain and could numb the leg.

† Against a smaller person: Moderate pressure is painful; a moderate blow could be very painful and a forceful blow is likely to numb the leg.

† Against a larger assailant: A moderate hand blow would have little effect. A forceful hand blow or a kick can cause considerable pain.

To deliver a penetrating blow, the extended-knuckle hand blow or an elbow blow would be practical. A toe kick would deliver penetrating force, but it is not a first-choice practical self-defense tactic.

KNEE. 48, 49.

The knee is a prime self-defense target area. It is vulnerable. It can be reached (by kicking) from out of
range of an assailant's fists. It can be used close in. It
can be used as a target from almost any angle and it is
available as an effective target for small individuals
defending against considerably larger assailants. Although
injury is a possible result, a knee injury is not life-
threatening.

The angle of the kick will affect the result. A kick into
the side of the knee is likely to unbalance or put an
assailant onto the ground. A kick into the front of the
knee is less likely to unbalance, but more likely to injure
ligaments and/or dislocate the kneecap (patella).

A kick made straight in at the knee, as shown in 48 is
more likely to cause injury. Delivered at an angle into
the side of the knee, 49, the kick is more likely to
unbalance.

† Equal adversary: A moderate kick at a 45-degree angle (approximately) into the side of the knee is likely to cause loss of balance and pain.  A forceful kick could tear or rupture the ligaments and/or tear cartilage.  Dislocation of the kneecap is possible.  Kicking straight into the front of the knee with force can result in severe hyperextension and serious injury to ligaments, cartilage and patella.

† Against a smaller person: A person of slight build is not more likely to be injured because of a kick to the knee due to the greater probability of being put on the ground rather than absorbing the impact in place.  A smaller individual held immobile and kicked into the knee would, of course, be in greater danger of serious and severe injury.  A moderate kick could result in injury to ligaments, cartilage and possible dislocation of the patella, if delivered at an approximately 45-degree angle.  A frontal kick of moderate or greater force could severely hyperextend the knee, resulting in injury to the ligaments and cartilage and dislocating the patella.

† Against a larger assailant: A forceful kick at a 45-degree angle can buckle the knee and put a larger person off balance.  There is a possibility of tearing ligaments or cartilage.  A forceful kick into the front of the knee could tear ligaments and cartilage and there is a possibility of dislocating the patella.

A kick into the knee.

A long-range kick into the knee, safely out of range of the assailant's arm reach.

## BACK OF THE KNEE. 50.

† A kick into the back of the knee, unless the leg is braced and unable to give with the blow, is most likely to result in buckling the knee and putting the individual onto the ground. Against a rigid knee, a kick from the back could injure cartilage and tendons.

From any angle, a stamping kick into the side, front or back of the knee is the most efficient technique.

Kicking into the back of the knee.

SHIN. 51.

On most people the shin area is peculiarly vulnerable to
pain. It is possible to bring about pain by merely pressing
onto this area and most of you will recall intense pain
resulting from accidentally bumping the shin. This is an
excellent self-defense target and particularly useful for a
smaller person defending against a larger assailant.

† Equal adversary: Moderate kicking blows result in
extreme pain. A forceful blow may involve a possibility
of fracture.

† Against a smaller person: A moderate kick results in
excruciating pain and there is a possibility of bone
bruise. A sufficiently forceful kick could fracture.

† Against a larger assailant: A moderate blow causes
pain. A forceful kick is very painful. It is unlikely that
a smaller person kicking a larger assailant would cause
greater injury than a bone bruise.

The most effective kick into the shin is made with the
edge of the foot or shoe; the thin edge of the kicking
surface results in penetration of force.

5 1

An edge-of-shoe kick into the shin.

INSTEP. 52.

The arched upper area of the foot is vulnerable to pain.
There are many small bones in the foot; a blow of
sufficient force to cause fracture could fracture more
than one bone.

† Equal adversary: A moderate stamping blow causes
considerable pain. A forceful blow could result in bone
fracture(s).

† Against a smaller person: A moderate blow is extremely
painful and there is a possibility of fracture. A forceful
stamping involves probability of fracture(s).

† Against a larger assailant: A forceful blow causes pain;
against a larger, heavier person there is no great likelihood
of fracture.

The stamping blow is an efficient technique. A kick into
the shin, followed by a scraping down the shin and com-
pleted with a stamping onto the instep is a particularly
effective defense combination.

A kick into the shin is followed through with a scrape
down the shin and a stamp onto the instep.

ANKLE. 53.

The ankle region is vulnerable to pain. It is also particularly susceptible to sprain.

† Equal adversary: A moderate or forceful kick results
in considerable pain. Fracture or sprain could result from
a kick of sufficient force.

† Against a smaller person: A moderate blow causes
considerable pain. A forceful kick could result in fracture or sprain, or both.

† Against a larger assailant: A moderate kick would
result in some pain. A forceful kick could cause considerable pain with a possibility of sprain. It is not likely that
a smaller person could deliver sufficient force to cause
fracture.

To cause pain, the edge-of-shoe snap kick would be most
effective. Used with sufficient force a snap kick could
cause fracture. A stamping kick could also be used to
strike the ankle target.

COCCYX. 54.

Commonly called the tailbone, this is the extremity of the spinal column. I do not favor this as a target area for practical self-defense. Perfect accuracy and considerable power are needed to deliver effective blows, which makes it a poor target for most people. If precision power blows are delivered to this area, there is a high risk of severe injury.

† Equal adversary: A moderate blow has little effect. A forceful blow causes considerable pain; a sufficiently powerful blow could result in severe injury.

† Against a smaller person: A moderate blow is painful. A forceful blow could cause internal injury, including damage to the spinal column and the spinal cord, with high risk of serious, irreversible injury.

† Against a larger assailant: A moderate blow has little effect. A forceful blow could cause pain.

A knee or toe kick is used to hit into this area.


BACK OF THE THIGH. 55.
A blow struck into this area is effective only if delivered with force -- using a stamping kick, for example.

† Equal adversary: A moderate blow causes some pain. A forceful blow is painful and could bring on a muscle spasm (charley horse) which is temporarily disabling.

† Against a smaller person: A moderate blow causes pain. A forceful blow is likely to cause muscle spasm with considerable pain. The probability of injury is minimal unless great force is used.

† Against a larger assailant: A moderate blow would have no appreciable effect. A forceful blow would cause some pain.

CALF. 56.

The fleshy area of the back of the leg just below the knee
is a target for foot blows.

† Equal adversary: A moderate kick causes pain. A forceful kick would cause considerable pain and perhaps result
in muscle spasm.

† Against a smaller person: A moderate blow causes considerable pain. A forceful blow might cause muscle spasm
and considerable pain.

† Against a larger assailant: A moderate kick causes pain.
A forceful kick would cause considerable pain.

The stamping kick or toe kick could be used.

ACHILLES TENDON. 57.

The long tendon which extends from the calf muscles to the heel bone is prominent and most sensitive at its lower extremity.

† Equal adversary: A moderate kick causes pain. A forceful kick would cause considerable pain with a possibility of injury to the tendon.

† Against a smaller person: A moderate blow causes considerable pain. A forceful blow could cause painful injury to the tendon or tear it.

† Against a larger assailant: A moderate kick is somewhat painful. A forceful kick causes considerable pain.

The edge-of-shoe kick is the most efficient technique; a stamping kick could also be used.

# SUPPLEMENT

## LOCATING THE TARGET

Depending on the season, the weather and the style of clothing, there are some target areas which would be somewhat protected, some target areas which would be altogether protected and concealed by clothing, and some which are likely to be exposed no matter what type of clothing is worn.

58. This illustrates the revealing/concealing characteristics of casual dress.

The head is exposed, as are the neck, wrists and hands. The casual shoes leave the ankle and instep exposed and available.

Other target areas would have to be gauged approximately. For this reason target points which require absolute precision to hit are not practical for basic self-defense for most people in most situations. The target areas which are practical for self-defense can be hit even when covered by clothing.

To hit the forearm nerve center, aim slightly below the elbow; the elbow joint is clearly visible in light clothing.

The knee, which is an excellent target for defense in serious assault, can be struck with reasonable accuracy even when covered. The shin can be struck at any point from the knee to the ankle.

In this type of clothing the solar plexus region can be located without difficulty. A blow struck slightly below the target is more effective than a blow struck too high.

58

In heavier clothing a scarf, collar or sweater might protect the neck, eliminating the side of the neck as an available target, but the nose is almost always exposed.

The shin can be struck through fairly heavy clothing; high-top boots would eliminate the shin as a target. Thick or high-top shoes would protect the ankle and instep.

Against vicious, life-threatening assault, the throat and eyes are ordinarily available as target areas. If the assailant were wearing glasses, the glasses could be knocked off as part of the defense action. Individuals who wear glasses regularly are handicapped and disoriented by their loss.

59. From the side, targets which might be available could
be the head and neck, the forearm, knee and ankle.

60. From the back, the side of the neck could be a
target unless it is protected by thick clothing. The back
of the knee is the best and most easily available target
from this angle. It is easy to see the wrinkles and
creases which show where the knee hinges.

## "BEST" TARGET AREAS

There are no "best" targets in an absolute sense. There
are different best targets for different situations. What
might be a good target area in one instance  might be
impractical, impossible or inappropriate in another.

It would be practical to  parry or strike at the arms  in
response to the reaching action shown in photo  61, but
clearly inappropriate for the situation  illustrated in
photo 62.

The defense action in response to the threat of assault
shown in photo 63  would not be possible in  the
situation shown in photo 64.

A high-risk-of-injury target such as the eye would not be
the best target for a  mildly offensive action but it would
be the best target in a life-threatening situation.

Ethical self-defense involves judgment of the degree of
danger and a choice of the appropriate tactic to deal
with it without resorting to needless violence.

61

62

63

64

## ACCURACY & SPEED PRACTICE PROCEDURES

The most common assault situations involve a smaller
person defending against a larger or stronger assailant.
For this reason you cannot rely on power blows unless
you spend a great deal of time training and practicing
to develop power.

For most people it is more realistic and sensible to learn
how to make appropriate, prompt responses to the *threat*
of assault and to learn the appropriate targets for hand
and foot blows delivered with reasonable accuracy and
speed.

*Look at the target.* Although this may seem to be
superfluous advice, it is very important. It is common
for most of us to look at objects without concentration.
It takes conscious effort to keep your eye on the target.

Practice by looking at objects to register fully their
shape, color, texture and mass. If you concentrate on
the *act of looking* it will help you develop precision
in hitting the target.

### HITTING A SMALL MOVING OBJECT

To improvise a useful and inexpensive training aid,
suspend a ball which can swing freely and can be raised
and lowered to face height and knee height.

This is a smaller target than you would ordinarily hit in
a defense situation. If you develop moderate facility in
hitting the swinging ball you should have functional skill
for striking a self-defense target.

65,66. Keep your eye on the ball. Practice hitting it with
a series of consecutive hand blows. Do not strike with
force; use a fast, light touch. If you hit the ball too hard
it will swing wildly.

65                                    66

Practice various hand blows. Practice hitting with your
right hand and your left hand. Practice to increase the
number of times you can hit the target with a series of
consecutive hand blows. In the beginning you may be
able to hit the target few times without missing. When
you can hit the ball with four or more consecutive blows
without missing you will have developed adequate and
functional skill.

Follow the ball with your eye instead of trying to chase
it with your hand.

67

67. With the ball suspended at knee height, practice
kicking at the target with various foot blows. Kick with
your right foot and with your left foot. Practice to hit
the target with light, accurate kicks. If you hit too hard
the ball will swing too far.

Follow the ball with your eyes and your feet will learn
to make contact with the target.

Another way to practice hitting a moving  target is with a
partner throwing a small beach ball.

In practice of responses to back attack it is important to
look at the target area.  Turn your back to the suspended
ball and practice turn-as-you-hit hand blows.  Practice
turn-and-kick foot blows.

68

69

## FULL-CONTACT STRIKING BAG

68,69. Full-contact blows can be practiced with a partner holding a striking bag. The training aid shown in the photo was improvised by filling a laundry bag with crushed newspaper.

Hit the bag with hand blows from different angles. Turn your back to the target and practice turn-and-hit hand and foot blows.

70

71

HITTING STICK

70,71. You can improvise a training aid by padding the
end of a broom handle or long dowel with foam or with
toweling. Fasten the padding with tape. For safety, do
not use pins or metal clamps. The padded stick can be
used to practice fully-released hand and foot blows.

72

HOOP STICK

72. Another improvised training aid can be made by
fastening a loop of wire about six inches in diameter to
the end of a dowel or broomstick. Do not leave sharp
ends of wire exposed.

As your partner moves the hoop around -- slowly, at first --
practice aiming hand blows into the center of the moving
target. As your responses become faster and more
accurate the training hoop can be moved faster.

## MEMORIZE TARGET AREAS

To prepare for those instances in which you might not be able to see the target clearly, you should practice to fix target areas in your mind as space relationships.

Assaults are more likely to occur in dark places than in lighted places. In dark or shadowy areas it is not possible to get sharp visual images.

Following are some practice procedures for memorizing body target areas.

73,74. Look at the target point and then turn away from it. Try to hit the target without looking at it. Space perception differs considerably from individual to individual; at first you may find that your perception of the location of the target is greatly distorted when you are not looking at it. Moderate practice should improve your ability to hit the target.

73

74

75

75. Mark a pole or stick with high and low target areas
at approximately knee and neck height. Practice
simultaneous hand and foot blows aimed at the exact
targets marked on the pole.


76,77. Practice responding to cues other than visual
ones. Blindfolded practice does not correspond  to
any particular assault; it is a training procedure   to
react to sound cues.

The "assault" cue is given by snapping fingers. When
you hear the sound, simulate a blow aimed at the
source of the sound.

76

77

FIGHTING STANCES:  WHY & WHEN

In most instances fighting stances are not practical or
possible for self-defense.

78.  The standard boxing stance, of which there are many
variations, provides a guard for the upper body  but the
lower body is unguarded.

This stance is quite appropriate for the sport of boxing.
The sport is played by rules which prohibit and penalize
hitting below the belt.  It is therefore unnecessary to
guard against low blows.

The terms  "low blow"  and  "hitting below the belt"
derive from the sport of boxing and they imply unfair
and unsporting tactics.  For self-defense, which is not a
sport and in which there are no rules,  low blows  and
hitting below the belt -- kicking into the knee or shin,
for example –  are efficient, practical and appropriate
tactics for a small person defending  against a larger
assailant.

78

WRESTLING STANCE

79.  When wrestling is played as a sport, the rules prohibit
the use of hand or foot blows.  Techniques are limited to
grappling and takedowns for the purpose of applying a
point-gaining hold.  Because of these rules there is no
need  to put up a defense against blows to the body.

The open stance of the wrestler is appropriate to the
activity.

But because of its open, unguarded aspect,  this stance
is not suitable for self-defense.

The parody of wrestling frequently seen on television is
not wrestling as it is played in collegiate, national or
world competition;  it is a show  put on to entertain the
viewers.

79

JUDO CONTEST STANCE

80.  Although in the past judo has been taught as a self-defense method, today it has taken its proper place as a sport; it is an event in the Olympic Games.  Like wrestling, judo is played by rules which prohibit and penalize hand or foot blows or any tactic intended to hurt the opponent player.

Judo players do not use a fighting stance because there is no need to guard against the possibility of being struck.

Contestants in a judo match are in close contact, gripping cloth of the uniform as shown in the photo.

80

## KARATE STANCES

There are many different stances taught in the various styles of karate. In traditional karate, stances are an important part of training and practice. For contest and tournament (the objective of most karate training) the stances are appropriate. It is my view that there are inherent drawbacks to karate stances for self-defense.

Self-defense is not a game. The purpose of using self-defense is not to win a point but to avoid becoming the victim of an assailant. If it is possible to accomplish that objective without fighting, so much the better.

There are many instances of threatened assault which can be handled and managed without any physical action -- verbal control and assertive behavior may be possible.

Taking a fighting stance eliminates the possibility of coping with hostility through negotiation or persuasion. It is easy enough to move from no physical action into physical action, if necessary, but it is very difficult to retreat from physical action once it has started.

Taking a fighting stance is a signal that you are ready for physical confrontation, that you are challenging the hostile individual and the action of taking the stance is more likely to provoke than it is to prevent.

In surprise situations, such as assault from behind, it is impossible to take a fighting stance. There may not be time to assume a fighting stance against a swiftly moving assault.

In those situations where physical confrontation is a possibility but not a certainty, I favor a guarded posture rather than a fighting stance. A guarded posture is any natural-looking position with your hands in front of you (ready to hit, if necessary) but not fisted, and with a strong stable foot position which allows you to shift body weight for kicking or for running!

81

81. This is the cat stance which is favored in some styles of karate. It is inherently a sport-fighting attack stance.

82. The horse stance, much favored by many styles of karate, is a strong and stable position. It is a good sport-fighting defensive stance.

83. This is a modified karate stance which offers high and low guards and permits quick shifting of body weight and ease of foot movement.

If physical confrontation is impossible to avoid, and there is time, and it seems appropriate to do so, a modified karate stance such as this one would be more practical than either the cat or horse stance. Or, you could take a boxing stance which has the advantage of concealing the style of your defense actions.

82

83

POINT TARGETS IN COMBAT SPORTS

The principal differences between sport matches and
self-defense are: In contest or tournament the players
are competing for points. They are usually of approximately equal skill and size. They have freely chosen
to be opponents in a game which has rules to be
observed by all participants.

Although the players in a sport fighting match might
be hurt or injured, that is not the main objective of
most combat sports. Even in boxing, a contest can
be won by demonstrating superior technical skill, style
and spirit -- without hurting the opponent.

In combat sports you can tell the winner from the
loser by looking at the scoreboard.

Point targets in combat sports need not be those
which are practical for self-defense. They may perhaps
be symbolic of body targets aimed at in hand-to-hand
warfare, but now modified for modern sport.

In fencing as it is presently played the point-gaining
targets are touched, not cut. Because of the rules,
the protective clothing and the objectives of the
activity nobody gets killed in a fencing match.

Kendo is an excellent example of a classic Japanese
combat skill which has evolved into a modern-day
sport. Like fencing, kendo is based on ancient combat
sword fighting. Today, a special stick made of split
bamboo (*shinai*) is used to represent the sword.

The players use protective clothing and gear. The
rules of kendo competition effectively eliminate the
possibility of injury.

Skillful kendo players in tournament are exciting to watch.
But the participants are enjoying the pleasure of physical
activity and the thrill of competition without inflicting
violence upon each other and without taking high risks of
serious accidental injury.

Kendo target areas are  onto the head, into the throat,
the side of the body or head, and onto the wrist.  These
areas represent lethal sword cuts at vulnerable body
targets.  But because a *shinai* is used to represent the
sword and the protective gear covers the head and neck
and the waist and wrists, the contestants do not hurt
each other.  Thus, an ancient war skill has been completely modified to meet the requirements of modern
sport.  Technical skill, body discipline and style are
demonstrated in kendo matches without risk of harm
to the participants.

## STYLES OF KARATE

*Karate* is commonly used as a generic term for the many
styles and substyles of Asian methods of hand and foot
fighting.  There are dozens of styles of Japanese karate.
Among the Chinese styles are  Shaolin temple boxing,
pa kua, kung fu (gung fu).   The Korean styles  include
tai kwan do  and hapkido.

Although all of the karate styles and methods use hand
and foot blows as the principal techniques, there  is
considerable diversity among them in  the manner of
training, in the selection of preferred techniques,  in
the emphasis on either hand blows or foot blows,  and
in their utilization of  prearranged routines (dances,
kata) as practice procedures.

Some styles of karate do not include tournament
training.  In the styles which do not prepare for contest
matches, solo practice and performance of one-man and
two-man routines constitute the training method.

In some karate styles there is competition which consists
of solo performance of routines to demonstrate  the
students' technical ability and formal skill.

There are other styles of karate in which contest matches
are used as the principal method of developing skill and
in which the training program is geared solely toward
preparation for engaging in tournament.

There is a wide range of rules and regulations among the
diverse karate groups.  As is true in other competitive
sports, there are a number of associations, none of
which recognizes the legitimacy of the others.  The
champion of one karate association is not regarded as
the champion by the others.  The objectives of the
various groups are also widely divergent.  There is one
faction moving toward dangerous, spectator-oriented,
sensational, exploitive matches.  Other groups are working
toward the acceptance of karate as a modern sport
geared to the health, physical development and physical
well-being of the participants.

KARATE CONTEST POINTS

The traditional, old-style karate point-winning target
areas are the most dangerous, high-risk-of-injury body
areas.  These targets reflect the original objective of
karate fighting for hand-to-hand warfare, as do the
target areas used in fencing and in kendo matches.
But in karate there are insufficient safeguards against
accidental serious injury.

The contest point targets in karate include head, throat
and midbody.  Some styles of karate allow the kidney
region and the groin to be used as targets.

Some karate contests award points for unopposed
blows which come very close to the target but do not
touch it.  The no-contact rule is supposed to prevent
injury.  Some karate contests allow contact blows but
require the contestants to wear protective gloves.  But
in both cases -- no-contact or contact -- the blows are
delivered into the unprotected, highly vulnerable body
targets.  Accidental or deliberate contact means high
risk of serious injury.

## KARATE MODERNIZED

If karate is to become a modern sport in the way that
kendo and judo have become modern sports, there
will have to be a change in the rules of contest.
Protective gear worn by the contestants has proven
cumbersome; it interferes with free and flexible movement. Clearly, it is the body target areas which should
and could be changed.

It requires as much skill to touch or hit low-risk-of-
injury target areas -- such as the upper arm, upper back
or shoulder -- as it does to make points by aiming at
the vulnerable areas now permitted in karate  contest.
Under the present rules accidental contact is dangerous.
Changing the rules would improve karate by reducing
the unneccesary risk without affecting the pleasure
and excitement of tournament play for the participants.

In no-contact.contest, points are
awarded for blows delivered very
close to the target area, if the
blow is unopposed by a blocking
action.  This would be a clear
point.

But accidental contact often
occurs because there is the
possibility that the opponent is
moving into the blow . . .

or because the players may
not have the high skill which
is needed for perfect control of
their blows.

When the target areas are high-risk-
of injury places, such as the eyes,
the absence of perfect control in
delivering close, no-contact blows. . .

results in forceful contact blows into
the most vulnerable parts of the
body. Accidental contact is
dangerous.

Accidental contact to a low-risk-
of injury target would reduce
the possibility of injury to a
considerable extent. If forceful
contact were made, it would not
have the effect of inflicting
serious, irreversible injury.

Instead of delivering a kick into
the groin area. . .

the upper leg could be substituted
as the target for point-winning
techniques.  There would be no
reduction of the required skill,
but considerably less possibility of
inflicting extreme and needless pain.

Kicking into the kidney and spleen region puts the
contestants  in extreme peril of dangerous blows....

When karate matches are played to entertain spectators
the only attraction is the promise of dangerous thrills.
Karate players who have prize money at stake may be
willing to play that game, but  physical education
teachers are not going to encourage karate  played as
a performance for a blood-thirsty crowd.

Highly skilled karate players do not *often* make the
mistakes which result in serious injury.  But most of the
people practicing karate are not highly skilled.  By
adopting new rules to ensure the safety of all the
players karate contest could be made entirely consistent
with the objectives of physical education and recreation
programs for sport, fitness and health.

Specific rules for any contest are made by the sponsor-
ing group.  There is nothing to prevent any school or
club from adopting health-and-safety oriented karate
contest rules immediately.

as does kicking into the head as a
contest tactic.

If the upper arm were made the
target point for tournament, the
sport of karate would become much
safer.

HEAD

A — FRONTAL BONE

B — FRONTAL SINUS

C — NASAL BONE

D — NASAL CARTILAGE

E — HYDROID BONE

F — EPIGLOTIS

G — THYROID CARTILAGE

H — WINDPIPE  (TRACHEA)

I — SECOND VERTEBRA  (ATLAS)

J — FIRST VERTEBRA  (AXIS)

K — OCCIPITAL BONE

FRONT VIEW
A – WINDPIPE                  E – LUNGS
B – CAROTID ARTERY           F – LIVER
C – JUGULAR VEIN             G – KIDNEYS
D – HEART                    H – INTESTINES

BACK VIEW   A – KIDNEYS   B – SPLEEN

SKELETAL/MUSCULAR STRUCTURE

A — STERNO-MASTOID MUSCLE
B — TRAPEZIUS MUSCLE
C — CLAVICLE  (COLLARBONE)
D — STERNUM  (BREASTBONE)
E — HUMERUS BONE
F — ELBOW JOINT
G — ULNA BONE
H — RADIUS BONE
I — PELVIC REGION
J — CARPAL BONES
K — METACARPAL BONES
L — FEMUR BONE
M — KNEE JOINT
N — PATELLA
O — GASTROCNEMIUS MUSCLE
P — TIBIA BONE
Q — FIBULA BONE
R — TARSAL BONES
S — METATARSAL BONES

## TENDONS, LIGAMENTS & JOINTS

Another category of hand-to-hand fighting is that which
operates on the principle of hyperextension -- bending ,
twisting (and sometimes striking at) the joints to force
them beyond the normal range of movement.  The effects
of hyperextension range from  moderate to extreme pain
and include the possibilities of dislocation, stretching or
tearing of the tendons or ligaments, and separation of the
connective tissue.

As with any  blow or tactic the results will vary with the
circumstances -- the force of the action, the relative sizes
of the individuals and the specific joint being hyperextended.

Aikido techniques are mainly  hyperextensions of the
wrist, elbow and shoulder joints.   When aikido partners
practice together, the  "defending" partner  will go with
the action or roll with it in order to avoid pain or injury.

However, if the aikido technique shown in photo  A  were
applied vigorously by a highly skilled individual against a
person who did not go with the action, but instead *resisted*
it, the combination of forceful pressure against the elbow
joint and a snappy twist of the wrist could dislocate  the
elbow or sprain the wrist, or both.

A

The ability to apply this kind of technique with the degree
of precision and the speed to make it effective can only be
acquired through years of training and practice and can be
maintained only with ongoing practice.

B

Many of the classic, old-style, traditional Asian self-
defense methods included (indeed, still include!) tactics
such as shown in photo B. In order to be able to apply
this wrist-twist/ arm blow combination against a
larger assailant, the smaller person would have to have an
exceptionally high level of skill.

But not all of the hyperextension techniques are as
difficult to learn and use as the ones shown in photos
A & B. There are some simple applications of hyperextension. The kick into the knee, discussed earlier in
this text is one example.

C

Another example is the easy-to-use, effective finger-bending action shown in photo C. With relatively little effort a finger can be hyperextended to cause pain and effect release.

D

For the lay citizen, control and restraint techniques like that shown in photo D have little relevance. Given proper and adequate training, professionals in law enforcement and related work can use them effectively.

# INDEX

BRUCE TEGNER is a specialist in sport and self-defense forms of weaponless fighting skills. He is regarded as this country's outstanding authority, teacher and innovator in the field.

He was born in Chicago, Illinois, in 1929. Both his parents were professional teachers of judo and jujitsu and they began to instruct him when he was two years old! Until he was eight, his mother and father trained him in fundamentals; after that he was taught by Asian and European experts. He began to teach at the age of ten, assisting in the instruction of children's classes at his parents' school. At seventeen, he was the youngest second-degree (nidan) black belt on record in the United States.

In a field where most individuals study only one specialty, Bruce Tegner's background is unusual. His education covered many aspects of weaponless fighting as well as stick and sword techniques. At the age of twenty-one, after he had become California state judo champion, he gave up competition to devote himself completely to teaching, research, writing and teacher-training.

In the U.S. armed forces, Mr. Tegner trained instructors to teach weaponless combat, he taught military police tactics and he coached sport judo teams. He has trained actors and devised fight scenes for films and TV. From 1952 to 1967 he operated his own school in Hollywood.

He has studied and researched human anatomy as it relates to sport and self-defense aspects of the martial arts and outdoor survival and rescue. He has taught first aid at the college level and he is certified by the American Red Cross as an instructor in cardio-pulmonary resuscitation.

Bruce Tegner has many books in print in his subject field. They range from basic, practical self-defense to exotic forms of fighting for experts. He is preparing new titles for publication and is revising and updating earlier editions. His books are used as texts for physical education classes, in recreation centers, by law enforcement training academies and by individuals throughout the world. Editions of Tegner titles have been published in French, German, Spanish, Portuguese and Dutch.

BRUCE TEGNER books are on sale at bookstores
and magazine stands throughout the world. If your
local dealer does not stock the titles you want,
you may order directly from the publisher.

For a free descriptive brochure, write to:

THOR PUBLISHING CO.
BOX 1782
VENTURA, CA. 93002